HOLD THE MUD

HOLD THE MUD

Poems

by

Yaneka McFarland

To my mother,

who I promised to thank in my acceptance speeches
but for now, this will do.

CONTENTS

"Either I must go home immediately and start to write or I must run away and start a wholly new life."

Henry Miller
Tropic of Capricorn

PRELUDE

In December I wrote
that the tragedy of Art
is thinking you can make it.

Saltwater

SALTWATER

brick by brick
she piles mortar and blood
there's salt in the water
where she builds with the mud

for traces of iron
of the Feared and the Bold
for those swimming with burdens
on shoulders that fold

a silent resolution
of children in men
wading white knuckled
for their mothers again

drawn to the deep
where dug toes let go
the bottom black dirt
lies barren to know

that to run through the battlements
with feverish flame
is to name laureled victors
who will wither the same

pockets will swell
start collecting silt
floating lungs fill

in gilded rivers of gold

A Short Death
runs ridges through the mud
A Life Transformed
where her metamorphoses spill.

UFO

She is a staple good
Pried Open for Judgement Day
Thrown under the eyes
Of mountains in men
She is an apocalyptic obsession:
The Undefined Female Objective.

She is a knight clad in armour
Stained with ruling blood
Running thicker than stoned walls
Under siege and broken
She is the guardian of maiden castles
A virgin's ticking clock.

She is a row of uncracked books
Waiting for eyes and softer hands
Yearning in dark corners collecting dust
A lone spine surrounded
With lines of Great Tragedies
An echo of the dead unkept.

She is a fly and the spider that eats it
poised on the wall of secrets
Egg shell whites and dirty linen
She is a predator
Praying without defense
Devouring her arcane deaths.

RIB EYE

I know you want to see me bleed
cut open on the page
I'll pull out my entrails
with a wide smile on my stupid face
standing in this butcher shop
behind my little glass case
serving up the meaty dead parts
for you to take all the way home
chop up in smaller pieces
and press down on your skillet
I'm burning until my blood runs
I'm cut open on the page.

FÉMININ

qui suis-je?
seule dans la rue
vide
sans peine
nue.

MILK FROM A COW MISSING FROM SLAUGHTER

jagged edges
and empty rigid words
carving into my skin

a pounding heart
fumbles drunk
over toothpick palisades

a shadow tails me

eats for me at breakfast
breathes from the ear of my chair
so I shovel temporary questions

spoonfuls into my mouth
stuffing it with anything
but his name

hemorrhaging

stop the bleeding with pressure!
so I press him until my thumb turns white
until it stops and I press a little more

picking at the scab
I watch myself bleed for him
I watch myself dig into my bones
until sorrow leaks thin

until I trickle into the pit of my stomach
until I am sick
until I am free

until I can eat slowly again
alone
letting him slip between bites

he's heavy
breathless
lost

nubivagant in the new air I breathe.

THE FOG

pulsing red
cigarette
butt

a
lighthouse
to lonely
sailors
coming home
under her
thick spell

cursed date
with the wind.

SEVENTEEN

he woke me with a sun
to cast us to the wind

we tossed and turned for days
and I held him by the hand

he pulled until it stretched
stretched it limp and bitter

I chose to face his walls
painting over the face it housed

I waited for thunder to crack
a white flash to strike me down

OPEN THE SKY I yelled
and he curled into the clouds

it poured for a hundred hours
and I drowned a minute short

his grip was wet with tears
his shudders shook the ground

I stayed in the passenger seat
'til the moon knocked on the door
she said kindly - go to bed
don't leave me please, he said

and when the ocean brought us home
I let him in again.

LOW TIDE

alone
a tangled place
sweet soothing friend
I spiral and dance
with crisp
crimson
petals
dawning on my nightstand
I am bedridden
foaming memory spills over
a sharpening brim
shackled
to wishful projections
to tides rising
to a celebrated blue
I remind myself that
the darkest waters
shelter the soft bottom
away from the
sun.

FRANK ST.

Saturday
behind white veranda doors
call it our last touch

not an early bird
still I sang for you

until the morning muted us

made breakfast lunch and dinner
the Last Supper set for two

my forked heart hit the plate
with the knife hid from view

eating a silence loud as god

bottles bottled a tempest
we left to brew but
champagne pours a golden truth

we knew so drink drank
drunk

Cheers to I Love You
sitting on the molding balcony
on the wall that we built
on our temporary elevation

splitting a cigarette
two stories high

speechless like we had the time

Sunday
the morning spent disguised
I'm in your door dropping eyes

at that place I saw you last
where we couldn't say goodbye

On Frank St.

VESTIGES OF YOU

he was my monday hangover
that lingered through the weak

A temple drum
that brought me to my knees

I was an atheist praying
for a resurrection of his affection
towards me.

THE CENTER OF A FLAME ISN'T ORANGE IT'S BLUE

I watch the candlestick
writhe
in its own hot
river

the blackened candlewick
reaches
grows shorter

I think
on the people who leave
like thinning
smoke
and the shadow that lingers
behind
that shadow that refuses
to die.

TINY DANCERS

grade school at twelve
I made acquaintance with death

two boys dressed in black
carried the news with her name

three words:
"she killed herself."

my heart fell to my shoes
laces turned to ribbon

I saw her starry tulle costume
under the lights on stage with me

a choreography of the night sky
she hid with darkness in the light

alone – I wondered where she went
if she believed in heaven or

just a room of her own
"The happiest girl" they said

I wondered about her often
and what the loneliest girl chose.

FLOWER SHOP POSTMORTEM

apartment flat
with a bottom store

roses line the windowsill
sitting still

are they breathing
or am I leaning in too close?

blink twice if you're alive
spell it out for me in red:

Open
lights, camera

bell
above the door

another loner enters
while outside it pours

sell her the size of love
in a tall gentle dozen

dethorned and pure
or perhaps a flowering cactus

wrapped up pretty

for her Saharan heart

tell her everything will be okay
and that'll be 38.95

have a nice day.

GOD, YOU'RE A TONIC!

you keep
the sheep
and wolves
awake at night

reading the tree lines
moving with the moon

your Sun
he's down here
hanging amongst the people

on grand walls with
bobbing voices
under mosaic glass

on fruit basket
wallpaper walls
by the kitchen sink
and under the clock

on silver and gold chains
strung around
believing necks

the people
they love him so much

that they eat
his body
and drink
his blood.

HOT SEAT

often
I'll go to the bathroom
sit down
push
and all that comes out
is a fart
and I wonder

am I becoming a prude?

Breakfast at Persephone's

A BRA CADAVRE

at 23
bras became the government
I could openly reject

a northern rebellion
from the brass
iron
wire
cupping my breasts

a frigid empty promise
of lasting youth
replaced with a few opinions
on the matter
of gravity.

ON THIS DAMNED ROCK

heedless sailors
mind their own
waving islands
in a cold
and shared
foaming sea
asking
is there really a maker to be met
housing sinful
drowning
dreary heads.

INSOMNIAC

heavy bones
       limbs of lead
she tells me
       eyes unfed
smoke rises, spills
       a skull cracks open
       I'm tired, she says

emptied basin
       a carcass head
she hangs her shoes
       three days in bed
abandon the search!
       send the dogs home
alone she's bled

idle hands
       marry the dead
she walks still
       on thinning thread
entombed in dependence
       presumed marriage
       of trust unwed

stale words
       satin pages unread
she scrapes the bottom
       of her undue dread

It's fine, she says
  digging a lung trench
  for a wider sea to spread.

VILLAIN

can you feel her in the shadows, friend?
She's clawing for affection
hiding in your shallow end

She feeds on the praise you send
gnawing on god's reflection
can you feel her in the shadows, friend?

her humble beginnings are all pretend
She's the hero to imperfection
hiding in your shallow end

starved for the limelight you lend
your rich and alternate projection
can you feel her in the shadows, friend?

She tells you no one can contend
it's your daily love injection
hiding in your shallow end

you're the world that She can bend
reveal: an empty introspection
can't you feel her in your shadow, friend?
She's hiding in the shallow end.

SUBTERRANEAN

the banjo players
play on their knees
stealing stolen letters
with painted fists

muddy water pours
from a golden tub
blood pools and stains
the marble face

expensive prison
or poor country club?
money in laundry bags
pulled with string

the safest deaths
are knit sunglasses
a dark white room
a corpse's box.

CHEAP MATTER

people talk
with eyes held
hidden in their mouths

a third globule
sloshing around
in the back of their throat
waiting

watching

smacking their lips
for the tail end of their letters
to lick the first earlobe
and find

juicy
agreeable
grey matter.

APPETITE

I can taste my misery

sitting at the crest of my forehead
hanging from my bottom lip

I see the words people speak
sentences welt my face

I amputate words in my lungs
before full-term implication

I can taste my misery

seething from my brow
seeping out splitting hairs

I feel the space around me shorten

a strange coolness closes in
cuts a clearing below the ribs

I can taste my misery calling
my company is hungry.

RED SWAN DAYDREAM

blood red dancers
swirl in my waking dreams
I can feel the pressure
in the arcs of my feet
crescent moons creeping back
pressing against the hardwood floor
my toes crack
where they used to glide silently
like the sea braces for release
a tidal role
rolling to its mortal peak
I remember how it felt
taking my foot out
from the wool in the pointes
still white – finally
no longer weak
I learned how to stay up
without having to bleed.

CLAIRVOYANCE

I keep a band aid
with the biggest knives in the drawer
just to keep
me sharp.

SATURDAY NIGHT ON YORK STREET

four drinks in
the idea busts in
cigarette!
we pile outside
        in my memory
        it's cold out
bodies shuffling close
puffing out smoke
and carbon dioxide
cut to
        three hours later
I'm lifting a burger to my face
in a much
too bright a place
with plastic seats
and friends that made it this far
        not in life, just tonight
        (but you can give them that too)
did someone say
cigarette?
we stumble outside again
        there's a loud laugh
        it lingers
I'm leaning on a shorter shoulder
a tighter circle forms
I see pairs
of shoes
a hand flicks

an orange lighter
a joint hovers in a circle
             it's morning
             but not really
we're running on delusions
kissing stick men
carrying the scythe.

NEEDLE PARK

eleven wooden slate benches
one with a man slumped
sleeping on it
large trunked trees
maple and thin
children on a gym
all jungle
no adults
concrete chess benches
no matches in play
plastic bagged
branches
passed by people with bags
holding poodle dogs and groceries
beer bottles
and empties
empty bags
roaming the side streets
the sidewalk chalked in pink
bold bubble letters
share a free blessing
a welcome sign
you might say:
"stay
safe."

UNDERBELLY CARETAKER

monochromatic drifter rides
the unseen on his feet
a sweet concoction of benevolence
and rising calamity
he pulls pavement sheets
stealing warmth in neighborhood
banks while you sleep

a retired gun without bullets
a pinch to ignore

he is no robbing hood

he is a cup bearer
to royal pennies in a paper chalice
the city – a glinting strip of bared teeth
his borrowed palace

he is the dream catcher
the warden of hunger
the unofficial doorman hunter
he is the forgotten soldier
and the high noon sailor
braving the rough western sea.

HARD TO KILL

maybe it's a girl
waking you from your sleep
neo-ethereal explorer
wade deeper
into this house of mirrors
where real strangeness
lies behind
and all the way through
country and dichotomy
evil genesis
and male genitalia
> (and don't you think
> that's such a pretty name
> for what we hide so hard)
tightly packed purses
bulging with coin
feasting our rise
on this bourgeois buffet
slaughtered with lamb
and a side of democracy
This Is Your Tomb
searing yellow flesh
rosy wallpaper
in a glass sized motel room
can you see them? come
rip out the needle
little hypochondriac
power up the UV

see how the freedom around you
turns green
under the purple blood light
of noble civility.

January

INQUIRY OF THE HEART

if I could touch
the coating of my heart
would it feel like
worn out sandpaper
used too many times?

would my pulmonary arteries
that jut out wickedly
poke fun of me when I breathe
when I give them the power
that they need?

what about
my great cardiac vein
would it drain enough of me
back into me to feel new
and the same again and again?

would my heart still pulse
through my pink and blue wrist
if I pulled it out slowly from my chest
if I laid it flat onto my open palm
would it recognize my face?

if I could pose these heavy questions
in my curious self-dissection
would it tell me, finally
what happens to my blood vessels

when this mighty ship goes dark?

ANGEL IN THE FLOWERBED

my grandfather
he built a house of rock
atop a rock
and put a red tin roof on top

it's the house that sits
on the corner of the intersection
overlooking red grocery stores
blue banks
and blue and white poutineries
that used to be fields
beaten paths and ancient trees

now the greenest patches
are short cut lawns
and leafy house plants
stirring in the wind

my grandmother

she kept the largest ferns
lady ferns
male ferns
and western sword ferns
shading the concrete around the pool
spilling through the fence

there were tulips out front

where the cars that passed would see
a breathing garden
asters and azaleas
peonies and petunias
and marigolds (maybe)
all beckoning for honks on
mere audacity

my grandparents

they had a guardian in the garden
but it didn't have a beard
or wear a red hat
or carry a stick
or wear big shoes
it was an angel praying
its eyes closed
praying
in the flowerbed they both tended to.

IT'S MY MOTHER'S BIRTHDAY TODAY

walking down Bank St.
to the Sunday farmer's market

my hands
cold in my pockets
Rambo's hands
rosy pink

we single file shuffle by a sled holding family

cross a one-way street

I blurt
hello!
to the homeless man on the corner
wearing fingerless gloves
he waves with his gloveless finger tips
"RIDER PRIDE"
he calls to us
a gap in his teeth
he points to Rambo's sports jacket
to the team on the back in green

we turn down the main strip
with the bagel shop
and the pizza shop in a duel
for the attention of bread

we walk the crusty side
the open sign blinking
over empty orange seats

my eyes dart to the red
wool mitt
lost in a haste
laying on the brick window ledge
a left
without the right
its little string cut
hanging out over the edge
little independent knit.

A DAY IN A LIST

coffee
bread
oatmeal and granola

coke
popcorn
the one for stove

get a microwave?

wine
cheese and bread
more cheese

diner
9V battery for the fire alarm

new toothbrush
coins for laundry
and call your grandparents already

"hello?"
"hi!"

goodnight.

PRUSSIAN BLUE PILLOW

"my mum is dying"

it was the first time
I heard it

out loud

that he said it
out loud

that something darker
caked his voice

my father's voice
didn't break
but I did.

ELECTROMAGNETIC

I watched the sun
rise orange
against the tiled pillars
of the window city
reflecting the gold
dipped
copper
of Morning
unrobing the colours
of Night.

PATHETIC FALLACY

it's too cold outside
to keep my window
open
to hear the rain

so I put on
my winter coat.

PRODUCT PLACEMENT

Colgate Toothpaste
makes me think of
his mouth
      brush
in the morning
in the mirror
      brush
brush
brushing and
smiling at me

SAINT PAUL STREET ON A BICYCLE

riding in a two-piece suit
through eleven o'clock drifters
pedaling down Place Royale
and Saint Paul street
with a brown paper bag
in a brown leather bag

A book
small and red
Romeo and Juliet
For 2.99

I'm at the door
ready to leave the store
the book in my bag
my brown paper bag
I pull the handle
the bell dings
and then I hear him read.

SOLIPSISTIC AFTERNOON

1 p.m.
and a few minutes passed

a cross country skier skis the length of the park
across the street

my coffee is cold.

I'm listening to a meeting
but I'm not
There
it's importance receding
pulsing away from the reality I create
"Working from Home"

I have no
microwave

My coffee stays cold.

the voices from the meeting
on screen
are moving jaws

I pretend I'm the skier

or the woman
walking her tiny dog

in his tiny red
jacket and boots
        and why do dogs always wear red?

I pretend I'm the man
sitting
reading on the bench

I don't believe myself

except the fact
that my coffee is cold.

12

Twelve is the house in the cul-de-sac
behind a tall pine tree
the one with the fire hydrant
the only place I call home around
my mother since I left
"I'm coming home."

Twelve is the purple striped billiard ball
that lanky red head stole from the bar
on my nineteenth birthday
where I forgot my wallet and never paid
and picked it up a week later:
unexpected money saver.

12 is a full calendar year
a full lunation of the moon
twelve is our god of changes
of contradiction and religion
and what Basquiat and Diaz meant
on the walls they sprayed SAMO
(same old shit.)

TUESDAY

young man in a green raincoat
taking his money-making fill
sifting crushed soda cans he's
dumped out onto the street

they sound like trailing fingers
set loose along piano keys.

SEVEN IN THE MORNING

draped winter trees
in brown burlap
pass in the train window frame
hunched witches in a frozen lurk

faceless heads wobble
in glass reflections
a cold shiver shakes
rattles the frosted window

silent doors slide
aside – a listless mob walks
walk, walk, walk
walk faster!

HYPOCRITICAL

A motel
pool
is taking a bath
with a trove of people
you've never seen

who all took a dip
a soak
a swim
in this lukewarm pit
that if you're lucky is

Outdoors

a chlorine bowl for
sun-soaked serpents
slipping in
shedding sunscreen shells
cooling themselves

but get in!

"The water is warm."

69

BURNING THE BREAD

sometimes
I rhyme
and I know I'm being lazy
I can tell
I reread it
I make fun of myself
backspace
backspace
backspace
an announcing drum
failure! failure!
whispers from the fourth wall
it tells me
it's getting late
just put an
end
to it.

PLATO'S ROPE

there is an astral plane
said to be above this cave
and a golden chain
for when we shed this material weight
an existential thread
waiting on the ascension
of the graceful dead
follow beyond over the horizon's end

a boat floats
anchored to this earthly shore
and the ethereal rope
stretches from its wooden bow
the tide laps on the wide aural haul
a bright moon pulls on the land
sinking the ships sailing
ignoble heads of man.

The Shores of Ithaca

ATOMIZED

I am a half body
half my heart pulsing
in the open air

I've seen her

The Vitruvian
Woman

she stands alone
circling unearthly shells

an apparition of colour
and translation
her shores are conditional
a conscious composition
a transfiguration of generations

she is a Page
to the Book of Visions.

VIVALDI IN A MINOR

a symphony wails
in the smoke in the distance

water rushes up from a fall
back into the sky

I see the wind in my heart
in the black coffee I stir
I am accompanied in obscurity

Obscurity (oblivion)

the day light casts riddles
as clear as milk

Obscurity (opaque)

green rolls of carpet hills
yawn under the prune night

Obscurity (twilight)

my Michelangelo speaks
from the pillow beside me

I am accompanied.

BASEMENT APARTMENT PARTY

It might have been ten
or two-thirty
I was on my bitter
last sip
with my glass tipped
back
looking at you through the bottom
talking animatedly in the kitchen
by the open fridge door
the little light flickered
you grabbed another beer
and tossed it into the room
to your friends standing
sitting scattered
mixing with mine
like moths finding new light

It was dark out
someone said the word
Park
and you already knew
my first and only question
you nodded
smiled
yes – there is an adult swing-set.

LIGHT OF THE LIME

shoulders pulled
my arms are a spring breeze
buoyant in the shade
of a peach tree
I am orange
and I am red
dancing for the yellow fire
that I need
beckoning with my hips
and the space between my knees
I am the applause
heels clapping patterned tiles on three
I am the lacquered centerpiece
and the name glowing from the marquee.

THE BULL: A HISTORY

when you go to New York
there's always
a head
or a hand
in the bull's ass
touching the balls
  (I was told that's important)
for luck
for financial prosperity

prosperity:

the bull was built
by a man named Arturo
a Sicilian artist
who arrived penniless in Brooklyn
in the nineteen seventies
and twenty years later
he wanted to say
thank you
for the open door

the gift
ready on December fifteenth
in the back of a truck
at seven thousand pounds
rolling down lower Manhattan
to an illegal drop

The Charging Bull

eleven feet tall
clanks down under
a Christmas tree on Broad street
a message
for the strong
to stay as such

then came the rich
a suited little snitch
from the financial district
calling for its removal

take the bronze bull away!
it's too poor
for our sore eyes

if only Arturo
had made it gold that day

but lucky for him
the passersby pressed
and the commissioner acquiesced
he gave the charging bull its place
where bowling green
splits from Broadway.

ROBERT PLANTED THIS

there's a crowd on screen
a blaring rock band
shakes the audience in the seventies

my mum
she turns to me
from the blue suede couch
tell me

"those shows were so good
you could taste it"

"they had a wall"
a wall of sound
speakers
"piled!"
playing into ribcages
and pouring out the ears

it was then that I understood
what I grew up with in the air
spilling out the stereo
drumming our dinner plates
crashing our pop parties
and topping my drinks

I rock on the rocking chair
pushing with my feet to the beat

my mum smiles at the rifts
without looking at me

if I am a puppet
these are my strings.

MIDNIGHT

my bowl of cereal
matches my mother's
two metal spoons
clink ceramic sides

her polar bear pajama pants
brush the wood floor

its nearly June

my bare feet
find the cool spots
between the couch pillow
and the arm crease

I'm listening to her talk
and chew
and nod
I'm nodding off

she's brushing her hair

my head is near the big windows
I can feel how wide they're open
through the gust sweeping in
slipping past my forehead

I hear wheels spin

outside on the slick streets
young drivers racing up
to the reach the old castle
sitting dark on the hill

my mother flips through channels
on the TV

my eyelids close
and tires screech.

GULLS OVER GREEN

the gawk
of a gull
brings the crash
of a wave
breaking upon a seashore
as if the rolling crest
was lead by a string
tied to a clip
clipped around the gull's wings

it's white round chest
surfing the breeze
swoops up
with a gust its wings expand
expulse the air and
bring with it
the lip of a wave's curve
pulling
thinning the water over
the slinking surface

like waving a fresh sheet
onto the bed.

BUDDY

he picks up
his acoustic guitar
pulls forth
the wooden stool
and sits
one leg
usually the left leg
propped high

he finds his tune

takes out the sheets
of lead recollections
steeped in melody

he looks at the
closest
far wall

and the cowboy
without a horse
sings

he's still got
his loaded gun.

A SWIM IN THE SELTZER SKY

in the lake
my limbs are a bow on a violin
gliding
through liquid sketches of white
bathed in blue
I am as light as lifeless
catching the light
crossing at meridian
and noon

deep reds crash
to orange waves behind
my eyelids
swathed
in a solar fire hymn
I am wading in a cratered mirror
my moving reflection
floods and falls around
my broad stroke mortal crawl

engulfed
a body of water
in a body of water
sparkling under a great
gaseous hue
I am a fish head
out of the water
watching carbonated clouds

with a new view.

THE BIRTH OF MICKEY FARLAND

a flying door
painted blue
whirls past my window

I'm in the bathroom

I pull the shower curtain aside
inside
a hundred butterflies
hover
flutter over the tub

a hollow alarm sounds
the shower starts
pouring warm

the cloud of wings is weighed
the window feels their pressure

it shatters
breaks
blows the whole wall away

but the tub remains

I climb into it entranced
my arms covered in sand

the alarm becomes a silent ring
dissipates with the hovering wings

the bathroom tiles crack
crumble
the concrete lets loose

I can smell salt
and black earth

a blinding tempest calls
calling through his salmon conch

I find myself surrounded
a valley chasing the sea
my bare feet make impressions
on the land

these Great Green Hills
they hold the mud for me.

Made in the USA
Columbia, SC
06 January 2022

53691658R00055